Florence

Sundress Publications

Copyright © Bess Cooley
ISBN: 978-1-951979-66-9
Library of Congress: 2024943661
Published by Sundress Publications
www.sundresspublications.com

Book Editor: Ada Wofford
Managing Editor: Erin Elizabeth Smith, Krista Cox
Editorial Assistant: Kanika Lawton
Editorial Interns: Addie Dodge, Isabelle Whittall

Colophon: This book is set in Halant

Cover Image: "Gravity," by William Pinkney Herbert, courtesy of David
Lusk Gallery, Memphis and Nashville
Cover Design: Kristen Camille Ton
Book Design: Tierney Bailey

Florence

Bess Cooley

for Monica

Contents

Florence

May Day and I've come home
a stranger to my grandfather.
The schoolchildren are twisting

tulips from tissue paper and pipe cleaner,
pretending they smell like tulips.

My grandfather tells me of the bunch of goldenrod
he's named Florence because he sees
a face in it. *Some things*, he tells me, *I make up*

for a little joy, but there is no
denying what is there. Still,

when he leaves home he kisses
the goldenrod goodbye. He tells me he misses her.
The children don't leave baskets

of tulips on our stoop like they used to.
My stranger grandfather asks me where I grew up. Here

in this house, though the kitchen's
been ripped out and replaced
since I've been away, though the room

my sister and I shared was repainted and filled
with my grandfather's furniture placed in the same

arrangement as in his house.
In his new bedroom, a whole desk
to hold one dictionary, a roll top kept
over framed pressed flowers,

his books glassed in.
He keeps to one side of the bed

like he's waiting for his wife
to end her long day, though
she's gone. He no longer

knows her name. Now only one
imprint in the bed when he rises.

Eight Years Old and My Grandfather Says My Name Angry

Instead I'd remember the Thanksgiving
we spent the day playing Heidi—you our grandfather

playing the grandfather, carrying my sister
on your back up our mountain
of basement stairs. You let me scout ahead
and break ground: the trailblazer.

Now I want to time-travel back to then, the day
you knew my name so well, even to hear you
say it angry. You could trace

the constellations with your hand overhead
and tell what they were called.
Show me the bright planets.

Now I look up searching for Jupiter
and the North Star, look down

at every rock, waiting for you to tell me
how sediment breaks down,

how to place our hands on bark to feel
the tree's age. I'd really listen

this time to what you called each layer of soil, to
Canis Minor, *Chinese gooseberry*, the little
climbing plant.

Corkscrew

Start late, pack
the essentials: bread,
two half-red apples, your
wood-handle pocketknife,
block of salty cheese, the bottle
of red wine. The knife

is corkscrew—we plunge the blade
as far as the neck will hold it,
spend the rest of that day on the trail

sucking on pieces of soaked cork.
By then I had a habit of trying to fly,
stopped at every cliff along the way,

though you, it turns out,
were afraid of heights. I took care
to line my toes neatly against the edge

above the blaring North Sea and spread
my wings though birds
will dive right off, they hardly know
the land ends. The apple cores I flung
over the side traced the arcs I'd spend years

trying to fit myself to: the trajectory
of flight. I graphed the jump I'd need
to get down that cliff without lifting

my wings. You uncap
your camera, say, *Spit out that cork*
before you jump. Could you make your arms
look less like you're on the cross?

Shuttle Gum

I'm standing with Kara while she has a cigarette
by the sweet gum tree, the secret smoking place
I never knew existed. *I'm killing you slowly,*
she says, *aren't I, with all these cigarettes?*
The sweet gum is covered in small knobs,
tumors climbing each branch. Kara and I
are talking about our butts, boobs, being naked
in front of our mothers, because butts, boobs,
nakedness usually come up when we're talking
about our mothers. The guy sitting next to us—
directly under the tree, its branches
clawing out to touch his face—he's also smoking
and gives that awkward laugh. He drops
his head between his knees and shakes it no,
though in this case he really means, *I can't believe
I'm hearing this.* Were I here alone, I would ignore him
but Kara says, *We're just talking about asses, how they don't
matter when you're a kid, you can show them off
whenever,* and the guy says, *Yeah, I have daughters,
they run around in panties all the time.*
Waves his hand. Wanders off.
To me Kara says, *Did you know this tree
went to space? It's called the Shuttle Gum.*
I look up to the bare knobs again. Kara looks to the ground,
which is supposed to have a metal plaque
hammered into it that tells us when, and where, and why—
and that would be sometime before now, and space, and
because the astronaut who did it went to school here—
but the plaque is covered in snow, just the corner
without words visible. Kara remembers somebody
rocketed the trees when they were saplings,
trying to discover how space affects growth,
or because they wanted to see if the seeds
would look like stars from Earth or grow on Jupiter.

The Shuttle Gum tumors suddenly seem not cancerous
but alien. I don't know if that astronaut
discovered anything or just
held the plants uncovered in his palm.

Moon Chart

I've discovered I was born
on the last quarter moon and spend all morning
trying to work out my fate. The Web
says *intellect and strength*. The other night

that moon eclipsed and reddened. *Blood moon*
bleeding softly in the sky. That night,
cloudy. I am sick of trying to figure out

what it all means. I wake now to a red sun
but do not take warning. My mother
tells me of her trip back home to Maine,
where all houses and their barns connect

in case of weather: house, front shed, back shed,
barn, all right in a row. *Sorry*, she says,
no picture, because she knows I want to see it.

She says, *All flannel and no frills—these are my people*,
which means they must be my people too, because
she is my mother and I came from her
and her people on the quarter moon.

I remember trails and mountains
and ocean. I remember her in the car. I do.
At my grandparents' place, I lie like a lizard

in their backyard meadow across two big boulders
and look at the sky. Both of them down there
with me telling me the moon's a sliver
winding back to new.

Dear Love Poem, Dear Memory

I've been writing love poems to my grandfather
who has started to call me *the poet*, the stranger poet.
He remembers the words to the old love songs,
sings them from his chair

to his stranger daughters, the songs of husbands
away at sea though he doesn't remember
that once he was the husband

away on a minesweeper
scanning the bottom of the Pacific for leftover bombs,

diving into the water praying
they wouldn't blow.
I'm writing love poems to the lemmings who hurl

themselves into the ocean, not suicide
or because everybody's doing it
but because they've eaten the land bare.

For my grandfather I write the family names
over and over as they dive

into the shallow sea: *Leslie, Deborah,*
your daughter, your daughter.

The names bob up from the surface—
anyone can see them for a moment—

then watch them drown.

Dear Love Poem, Dear Memory

my
             stranger

scanning   for leftover   s,

but   bare.

over and over

             for a moment−

Hemoglobin

For four months I lived
with three different strangers'
blood in me. All one night

I watched three people drip into my arm.
I didn't name them. Then I did: Owen, Gloria,
Oliver. I got to know them

so well we could communicate.
We went through our days together:
I sat at cubicle desks with them,

monotonously typing. Their blood
plowed through me.
Now I forget all three, but the signs

are coming back—motion sickness on the bus,
dizziness climbing out of the pool.
I check them off like a doctor's list, think,

my hemoglobin's probably at 9, now 8.
I take iron pills but think every time
about letting my count go back

down, letting myself come in
and out of the world. Sometimes
I want to remember the people whose blood

I shared, but my body didn't know
it was borrowing from them, who
went to the blood clinic,

sat in medical chairs, ate cookies, drank orange juice
after giving it away. My cells didn't

think of ownership. Poor, forgotten
Gloria, Oliver. My body drank and drank.

I've Had This Rhythm in My Head for Decades

My mother at the sink trimming beets,
my mother at the sink peeling onions.
The day she learned to pull the seed
from an avocado by wedging

her knife in and twisting the knobbed pit
from the fruit, even her chopping blade
quickened its pace—liberation!

When I was in the hospital,
her rhythm slowed back again

for me, matched the drip of strangers' blood
into my IV. I asked, *How long*

until my blood's mine again? Four months
working the blueprint of strange cells,
four months with a borrowed pulse, but even

my chopping is my mother's
chopping, my walk my mother whispering
into my ear like a prayer
heel-toe, heel-toe, heel-toe.

Poem Starting with a Violin and Ending with the Hoan Bridge

When my grandfather died, he did not suddenly
recognize our faces at the end of it all.

When I called, my mother did not say *Come home*
or *Skip the rest of your class and rest*

but *Do you think you can pull yourself together?*
The children in the after-school

writing class I teach are killing every character
and bringing each of them to life again: *The robot*

broke down and then it came back alive.
We waited to write what we remembered

of him on a piece of posterboard.
There was *Stargazing* and S*hoveling bats*

out of the chimney. The time we went backpacking.
Learning to write with pen and paper

seems these days a dying art, children
learning only to sign their names in cursive.

The time he tracked its orbit and followed
Jupiter home. The time he...

I dream we give my grandfather
the pen and he does not write

of his German violin or how to build a perfect fire.
But he remembers the names of every

constellation, the way
stars move. We burn

the memory board in the fireplace
and mix it into his ashes in the pine box on the table.

Only children with a name
starting with L will learn the curls

of that capital letter, trace the loops
backward and forward, practice

where they might make the two
loops intersect, a purposeful,

impermeable third loop.
Workers are rehabbing

the bridge in Milwaukee
that took me to my grandfather's

one room and to his nurses
those last few

months. The construction men
have a deadline, so

they rebuild even in the snow.

Poem Starting with a Violin and Ending with the Hoan Bridge

Come home

remember

                    the way

        memory

                        loops
              backward and forward

    one
                last

        rebuild

§

To the Person Who Signed My Name on the Backs of Checks Written Out to Me

You did it more carefully than I.

In September drove up to the window,
said, *This is me*, and the bank

believed you, handed you cash
through the sliding tray, counted it out

in 20s. Maybe you asked them to break it.
We all need small change, you know.

You signed so beautifully, slight curl
at the top of the C and two O's looped,

the E mellowing into the Y.
I want to see you write my name

on the security footage the police
told me they had. And when I watch

the tape I'll say, *Yes, those
are my hands signing*, veins and calluses

in all the right places, first, second fingers
and thumb holding the pen

dusk–paced in that transitory
glow of something leaving.

The cops won't have to bring you in
and I couldn't pull you

out of a line-up where all the women
look like me. I get

why the bank thought you were
me, or some better version. And I've already

told them we're the same.

Peter and the Wolf

I listened to the music on the radio this morning
and afterward every sound on the walk to the bus,
each sound in the day seemed to be played

by some instrument. Flute transforms
to bird, the bassoon to grandfather
(the one you already know),
oboe becomes a duck. Rain scattered like a snare drum

that morning and when I dove into the pool
cymbals clashed, then underwater

a muted French horn, a musician's hands
cupped around the bell. It wasn't that the world

was suddenly a symphony
and I the conductor, or that each person I encountered
in the day played a duet with me, my love

the euphonium humming trills into my ear.
It was more an orchestra warming up,
each of us in our private corners playing our own
most difficult passages, closing

our eyes, feeling it in the fingers, marking reminders
in pencil on the score.

Layering

So the other night I'm in class
and the teacher is talking about
layers. How we put them on, take
them off, etc. Then she peels off her skin.
Underneath she's huge boobs, smooth crotch, legs
on hinges. I follow a student home. He has
a workshop of some sort. Little machines that could
make anything, but human hands spring
out of them and carve birds
from cedar blocks. They move slowly and brush off
the shavings. I spend the next morning
trying to remember what
the workshop contained. Which tools.
How large the blocks of wood.
That student doesn't want me to come in. *It's*
private, he says and I get it. I too
want to stay in my skin. Two days
later—and this is real life—I'm sitting
in a room with this poet who is talking about
writing. *It's layers*, he says. *Not*
even the poet understands what's
underneath. Then he peels off the skin
of the room. It fills with water.
The windows break and we
remain sitting. In that flood we swing
together like hanging plants.

There Is a Snake

This isn't a metaphor. And I'm
not the snake. He was really there,
then slithered into the short grass,
under the bushes that to him
must've been enormous, good
cover, then into the small forest
where I couldn't see him.
So I continued along the trail.
Here, I might as well say it:

I pushed him off the path.
I was worried a bicycle
would gut him. I grabbed
a stick and sent him. I still want to let him
just be a snake.
What else could a snake want?

Mice, water, underbrush, somewhere
to hide, a hole to carve out
channels, span the length
of this brush, narrow
dirt capillaries to explore...
And what could I give him

but a poke? I said I wasn't
the snake and it's true. When I slither
under the grass I crawl along
on my arms. While the snake
disappears, you can see much more
than the outline of my body.

The Summer I Begin Having Seizures

A squirrel shivers up the tree, his shadow
shivers after him. I think he sees me,
slinks his fur down to bark-level.
On the hill on my porch it may look
as though I'm sitting in a tree,
surrounded by old oaks and bushes, a family of birds
living there, nest of many twigs
and hair—probably mine—and another
larger nest in the tree grown above
my big, white house, so I can't see anyone
pass on the sidewalk. Not the short man
carrying his tall boombox on his shoulder, swinging
to its beat or the man who lives
across the street with his two loud
dogs, his banging on the screen door
to quiet them or the kids who coax
caterpillars onto leaves with their grubby hands.
I have done this on purpose.
On purpose I've moved my chair to sit
behind the high bushes. On purpose
I drink my tea on this porch
each warm morning, angle
the chair, and bring things to read
on purpose, mostly conversations
between writers who tell each other
their successes: books to be released,
their good writing habits, hunkering down
for hours each morning,
mug of tea in hand and clacking away.
Suddenly the squirrel.
He has shimmied along
the branch and I've moved
my legs so they may not be seen by traffic:
loud motorcycles gunning their engines

which sound like shots,
chugging their way up this high hill.
The squirrel and I,
we are nothing alike. We eye
each other hiding.

The Other Side

Earlier today the dogs sprinted around the yard.
Chasing squirrels and birds.
They went too far. I couldn't see them.
I cut through brambles to look for them.
I walked to the other side of the forest.
I was barefoot. My feet calloused into leather button-up boots.
I broke out in another century. Or world.
I couldn't tell. I was only looking for those dogs.
On the other side were purple mountains, a yellowing ocean.
I had thought I was in the Midwest.
Yet this was no ocean of corn.
I swam it. In the Philippines I rested.
For a while. Then went on to China.
Around India I swam for those dogs.
Suddenly I remembered they both hated water.
They would run from waves that came too close to their paws.
So I swam back and was out of breath.
I sat on the hardwood floors of my house.
My dogs were there. I cried. I thought it was relief.
Who knows what it was.
The dogs licked my face. Who knows what it was.

Peter and the Wolf

every sound

transforms
to grandfather
(   )

difficult   closing

Off Season

In April I make hummus with lentils and use too much
water and not enough lemon juice. It's that weird
winter-spring space. I do not go outside. When I do,
I dress in layers: long-sleeve t-shirt, sweater,
lined puffer jacket. My parents are leaving the country again,
meanwhile my grandfather stays crazy and forgetting.
They lay out their shampoo and face soap in 3-ounce tubes
lined up in quart-size plastic bags,
pants with shirts on top of them, outfits
planned according to schedule—only what they need
folded neatly into backpack pockets. This spring
I'm the unneeded layer. My grandfather
hallucinates bands of witches calling him
from the trees. He sees them but won't look at me.
If you haven't worn this jacket in a year throw it
out of your closet. If I'm not useful to have around in spring
keep me packed in a box. If only I were
a winter parka I'd be an everyday necessity for my grandfather
at least another month even when checking
the mail or taking out the trash.
He would sew my name into the back of my neck.

New Medicine

Kate reminds me of the old seizure experiments—
drilling holes in their heads, removing
cerebellums, how doctors discovered
short-term memory there. I scroll through articles
she sends me—so many medical terms for what feels to me

just like shivering, then falling asleep. Under the MRI
machine I imagine it: the small flaps of my skull
siphoned away, a doctor flipping each
open like a latch. Would she say, *Cured?*

I cut pills in half over the green
plastic board, knifing the small indentation in each pill.
Even halved, they leave me muscle-tired.

The pills are dulling my brain. Which is exactly
what they are meant to do. Someday someone will say,
Can you believe they used to do that to people, drug
the entire brain? Someday someone will find these pills
I take twice daily, for which I set phone alarms

to remind myself, useless, just imprecise medicine.
I'm beginning to remember how similar meds
dulled my sister, made her sleep nearly twenty years
ago. A child with the brain's
extra firing and only one way to stop it.

Florence

pretend

My grandfather
                    sees
        Some things

    a little joy, but
                    Still,

    he leaves
            He tells me

            the room

            kept

    glassed in.
He keeps

     He no longer

       Now only one
imprint

For My Mother, Afraid of Forgetting

after watching her father forget it all,
history seeping out of him like water

through two cupped hands. He named
a sprig of goldenrod an arbitrary *Florence*
and made way for that name
in the space for names, letting go

of ours. My mother brought him home,
painted the walls pale green for him, balanced
his old furniture around the room. He said:

Thank you for rescuing me.
My mother says: If this happens to me
shoot me or better yet take me

out to the lake, over the bluff,
set me up with a bottle of single malt in the coldest winter,
lay me down in some

snow cocoon, lay me down
if ever I forget your face.

§

Two-Day Drive

Sky the way it is now, pink
and blue striped baby's blanket.
Trees nuzzle their nakedness

against it. Just the other week
we drove across country
and noticed those winter trees.

They might have been more
beautiful for having no leaves.
You driving, teaching me

southern stories: ghosts, bogs.
Me, just trying to keep you awake.

I say your South is this
sky blanket. My Midwest

the tree branches and you're
over here keeping me warm.

Last night the dog curled between us,
had some dream and barked
and barked. Toward the divide of him

each of us reached out to touch his head.

For My Mother, Afraid of Forgetting

He named

My mother

He said:

the lake

some snow
your face

MRI Music

What music I'd like?
I say, *Classical*,
which the technician
forgets to turn on.

Because I'm listening for
Schubert which never comes
I hear tones
in the machine's beeps and clicks.

Try to follow the rhythm in the way
it jolts my shoulders.
I will my head
not to move inside that big tube

as asked. I can't name
the notes but still
they seem to follow
some harmonic pattern.

They seem consequential, planned.

Elegy

In England for the week, I learn
my kindergarten best friend died.

He came to my all–girls–but–him
fifth birthday party

and sulked. Maybe I told him
there'd be more boys. Or he didn't like

the folk singer who came to sing.
At school we played
what kindergarten children play: ball, tag,

house. The play kitchen, kid–sized frying pans
and hamburgers, hot dogs

that snapped into their buns.
We pretended to have a life
together, nom–nom–ing

on plastic at a shared table. Children don't think
that it's hard. People are saying

he took pills or overdosed. No one knows if he did it
on purpose. I'm not sure how that poison goes—
slow slink into the blur? Or hurling

days into a toilet, eyelid capillaries breaking?
The day I hear his name for the first time in years

is the day of his funeral.
I should be sitting in the hard pew,
struggling with Catholic hymns I don't know,

shaking his mother's hand, his father's. But I'm here.
At the Tower of London crawling

the stone cells with the ghosts
of Edward IV's boys. I'm circling the courtyard

where Anne Boleyn put her head
carefully on the block.

Family Farm, Maine

The farm where my grandfather's father
was raised, where my grandfather may have spent
a childhood summer or two,

no longer stands. It has crumbled
and in the picture my mother sends: stone gate

with a carved sun setting over the farm.

Or maybe it rises. Below it the Ten Commandments printed
on stone and worn. I can make out, THOU SHALT NOT
MAKE GRAVEN IMAGE. The picture's sky

is cloudy. Mountains
rise. Those must still exist

even if not the white house, the wood barn. No graven image
could remind my grandfather of this home, of Maine.
His plaques and tangles like ivy crawl,

covering bricks, digging in, cracking mortar.
My mother says, *I disappeared along with him—*
my childhood and life no longer exist.

Elegy/Family Farm, Maine

He

crumbled

or maybe

snapped
We pretended
The picture
together
shared

No one no
home

days   breaking

His   tangles like ivy crawl,

I disappeared

I'm circling

Poem Written While Waiting for the Doctor to Call

I'm hearing this city in musical parts.
Here is where the parking garage lights up

and whirs in spite of itself. Here are two people
comparing heights and the man says he's only

taller because of his hair. Here is the part
where the girl at the table next to mine

takes a selfie with her iPad, trying to be discreet
about the tablet's click, lowering the screen to just

below her ribs, slightly away from her body.
She doesn't pout. I want her to hashtag the picture

TryToGuessWhatI'mDoingRightNow or *TheStreetlights
AreTurningInStagesAllAroundMe*. I imagine the streetlights

a soft snare drum when they blink. I assume
the girl does not turn, but the world must, like a radio dial.
That fuzzy warble. Sleet hitting the sidewalk.

An Archaeologist Shows Us a Skull

says the bottom bulb's *full blown*,
calls it *bun*. It's ancient. Only a few
months ago my neurologist showed me

scans of my sinus cavity,
the sphere of fluid nestled there, probably
not growing. This was the not−

dangerous cyst. He said *sensitive,*
overactive, any pain, lots of headaches?
I told him no before remembering

rising in airplanes, how
the top of my nose and my eyebrows
feel like a tightened metal rod.

And every time in diving wells I stop myself
suspended under pounds of water:
Don't hit the bottom. That cavity thrums.

An Archaeologist Shows Us a Skull/Dear Love Poem, Dear Memory

scans of my sinus cavity,
the sphere of fluid
        This was the not

            remembering

        he was

diving into

                the land bare.

            my grandfather
over and over

into the shallow sea

                surface

        drown.

§

On the Chicago River

Buildings sway on the glass sides of other buildings.
My tour guide talks post-modernism,
says such a structure copies
what surrounds it: the curve of this tower
following the bend in the river,
same height as the concrete warehouses nearby.

All week my brain has been processing
images itself. On the MRI scan there's an empty space
where it looks like a part has been washed away
by waves. It's a pouch of fluid
old as I am, full of water as I am, to be

sucked out by a tube, carried away to a place
that is not my head. Buildings are constantly

in relation to their surroundings—
the prairie grass next to the river, the high banks.
To the styles that came before. To me,
even, since I can see my wild hair,
my old tee-shirt in their window glass.

In the train station this morning
I took the doctor's call. He told me
the name—*arachnid cyst*.
The buildings wave at me with their pinched edges.

I have a spider in my brain.
It crawls along the left side.

It skirts the tricky bottom
of the cerebellum, that ball balancing
the larger beast. I look to the top

of what is no longer
the Sears Tower. The warehouses
around it are no longer warehouses,
now apartments, iron porch
railings chained to their cream brick.

No longer the warehouse
clatter they made—squeaking
grain elevator pulleys, thudding sacks
tossed to the ground, steamboats chugging
upriver delivering their no-longer
wheat and lumber. And my brain

no longer my brain. I'm no longer
a child looking up, thinking I'll live here,
write for the *Chicago Tribune*,
no longer have to imagine my life.

My spider tickles one leg against
what will become my memory
of this day. It is spinning

out its web, first the interior shapes,
then outward to larger spirals. They wrap up
the part telling me where my feet
must place themselves, on what portion of the heel
to lay my weight—wrap it up as prey.

I understand this is not how bodies work.
The cyst is always in the back of my mind.
In my brain, it lives up front. *Look at that skyline*,

says the tour guide. *Take
some pictures*. I snap with the cyst
lens of my brain. Has it always been there?

Maybe this is how I see things—
through this bubble, as if glass.

Afternoon

I don't mind sunlight there. Really,
love when it moves across
the dust, slowly makes it glow.

This isn't only because I don't
want to vacuum,
though I do hate the sound of that machine

and all my furniture
scraping the floor.

Afternoons when the sun hits
I can trace what I've tracked in—

gravel from my shoes,
dirt, the single
long blade of something

from the yard, bent,
so delicate it must be broken.

In the Library Just Reading a Poem

Here strangers keep me posted on their doctor visits
and I recognize the other library goers now
by their ailments, the only
thing I know of them—old football
injuries that lost one a college
scholarship, or the woman
in reference, next to the maps, with brittle bones
who should have gone
to the military but first
to fat camp. *Fat camp*,
she says, *I should have gone there too*.
She asks if I know a thing
about computers. *Sorry*, I say,
I have a Mac. But it's like learning a language:
she'll have to practice every day. My teacher once
made us write without picking up our pens
like we were learning cursive, learning to not
cross out, which—whoops—
I've already done in this poem and I've
done worse. I've erased.
No trace of the old
thoughts left on the library table
littered with pink
eraser crumbs where I'm brushing
them off and reading the poem whose page
has torn just above *An Elemental Rust*—

Poem at Seven O'clock

At this point I'm sick of my grandfather.

Outside, the branches bare.

There is not enough firelight in his old clay brick fireplace.

He takes out his pocketknife.

He sharpens my colored pencil as he has for years, navy blue.

The tip bears through, struggles out of the wood.

Leaves in its wake the shavings.

He has old hands.

Remembers when all pencils looked like chopped down forests.

He tells of his mother, a maid.

Once she held her boss's crying child and was fired for it.

The fire continues to die, he continues to not yet.

But it is fall and the world is ending.

So our ancestors thought one thousand years ago, he taught me.

They were tricked into Jesus by celebrating the return of light.

So let's have a party!

He is old enough to have ancestors.

His ancestors are mine.

A Murmuration
of Starlings

Other passerine birds, which means perching birds,
which means songbirds, which means birds
that copy human speech, may join the pulsing flock,
more physics, more the wings
of one starling turning into the wings of the next, more the air
turning between their wingtips
than evolution, as a whale rising,
as an ocean, this system poised to tip,
a hovering black wave.

On the Day My Parents Leave the Country They Leave Instructions for What to Do After Their Deaths

Call the accountant. Sell the house,
we've arranged for that money
to be sent to you directly, share

half with your sister, choose the cheapest
coffin for burning. Here, a list of people who will help you:
former guardians, the accountant again, his number in the file.

Which does not tell me where to mingle
my parents' ashes, to bury them, to plant

a tree overhead like we would grow above
my grandfather—my root-father pitting

himself to the ground, small skinny
mother re-growing her green

arms. I'd cut blossoms from her
and keep them, scissors angled against the stem.

The Furniture Room

I asked for a table and was given a key
to the room of tables and chairs
and a standing whiteboard,
no dry erase markers but a written note,

small page torn out with her name
on it, the woman who gave me
this key. I can't make

my way through all of it, the desks
piled on top of each other,
chairs balanced on each of them.

I didn't want anyone outside to see
the trove I found. To which
I was given this key.
When I had to give it back

the door locked automatically
behind me. No way back in.

My Mother Asks for Advice about What to Do with Her Father's Ashes

Her sister says that ashes these days
can be made into anything—a diamond,
or shaped as a coral reef and placed

in the ocean for sea urchins and fish to live in,
sand dollars, starfish, for seaweed to grow over

my grandfather, to cover him, for fish to lay new eggs.
How small his body could be compacted:

to one pearl. My sister tells us you can make
a tree—the bone-white ashes growing
into green, supple branches,

little blooming buds, oh,
I will visit every day until they open.

The Day My Parents Accept an Offer on My Childhood Home

is the day after they put it on the market.
        The realtors' pictures didn't

        look like home. They kept
nothing we had in that house where

my grandfather stayed,
        where before he fell asleep

        each night each of us made sure
he didn't need anything,

then turned off the light.
        But days later, looking again, I see

        they did keep one thing of ours
in that bedroom: the comforter

my mother picked out when my grandfather
        came to stay for good. Gray,

        thin stripes. The realtors
must have liked it for its perfect

neutrality, because to them it didn't say
        here someone lay

        while neurons in his brain mangled.
They didn't see that brain under the machine.

I decide the headboard
        must be fake, the plant

        sitting on the radiator, silk.

Pillows, throw blankets all fake, then

the comforter, the stripes.
      It stays there in the spot

      where it warmed my grandfather, where he turned
under those same beams, above those floorboards

and outside in the doorway in the corner
      of that photograph I listened to him breathe.

The Day My Parents Accept an Offer on My Childhood Home

he fell asleep

he didn't need anything

                              where he
turned

                         I
    breathe.

Florence/The Day My Parents Accept an Offer on My Childhood Home

I've come home
to my grandfather.

that house where
he sees

a little joy
where   he fell asleep

each night

he kisses

the comforter
my mother

his house

here

keeps to   the bed
stays there

warmed   he turned
above those floorboards

and outside in the doorway

Acknowledgments

Thank you to the following journals, in which several of these poems were first published: *American Literary Review; Atticus Review; Breakwater Review; Forklift, Ohio; Iron Horse Literary Review; The Journal; Midway Journal; Mississippi Review; Prairie Schooner; PRISM; Ruminate; Stirring: A Literary Collective; Toad;* and *Western Humanities Review*.

"In the Library Just Reading a Poem" ends with a line by Emily Dickinson.

Thank you to all the readers of the many drafts of these poems, especially Lauren Mallett, Alex Mouw, and Anthony Sutton. Thank you to those who generously read and discussed the full manuscript with me, sometimes several times over: Hannah Benning, Katie Condon, Allison Davis, Jeremy Reed, and Anthony Sutton. Thank you to Ada Wofford at Sundress Publications for their close editorial eye. My teachers have helped me make this book, especially Monica Berlin, Mary Leader, and Don Platt. Without Marianne Boruch, teacher, mentor, and advisor, this book would not have had a hope of existing. Thank you.

Finally, thanks to my family, who gave me not only my love for books but reminders to look outside of them. Most especially, thank you to my husband, Jeff Amos, who taught me about narrative, and much more than that, exactly when I needed it.

About the Author

Bess Cooley is a winner of the *Mississippi Review* Poetry Prize and her work has also appeared in *Prairie Schooner, Western Humanities Review, American Literary Review, The Journal*, and *Verse Daily*, among other journals. She is co-founding editor of *Peatsmoke Journal* and teaches at the University of Tennessee, Knoxville.

Other Sundress Titles

Back to Alabama Valarie A. Smith $16	*Good Son* Kyle Liang $16
Where My *Umbilical Is Buried* Amanda Galvan-Huynh $16	*Slaughterhouse* *for Old Wives Tales* Hannah V Warren $16
Grief Slut Evelyn Berry $16	*Nocturne in Joy* Tatiana Johnson-Boria $16
Ruin & Want José Angel Araguz $20	*Another Word for Hunger* Heather Bartlett $16
Age of Forgiveness Caleb Curtiss $16	*Little Houses* Athena Nassar $16
In Stories We Thunder V. Ruiz $16	*The Colored Page* Matthew E. Henry $16
Slack Tongue City Mackenzie Berry $16	*Year of the Unicorn Kidz* jason b. crawford $16
Sweetbitter Stacey Balkun $16	*Something Dark to Shine In* Inès Pujos $16

www.ingramcontent.com/pod-product-compliance
Lightning Source LLC
Chambersburg PA
CBHW031006090426
42737CB00008B/700